BODY LANGUAGE READING:

The ultimate guide to quickly
read people's body language.

Oliver Bennet

Table of Contents

Chapter 1:   First Impressions

First impressions are typically accurate. You should listen to your gut.

 Your subconscious mind is adept at picking out clues about people that your rational mind cannot pick up on. Your gut will tell you the most accurate information about someone right off of the bat.

After you make a first impression, you may try to rationalize it. You may try to explain away negative feelings as poor judgment or jealousy. You may think that you read a person wrong. While these are vaguely possible, you will usually find out that your first impression was right in the end.

A good example is when you first meet a woman that you would like to be friends with. But your gut reaction to her is that she is not very nice. You decide to give her a chance since everyone else likes her and you get along after a while. However, after a while, you realize that all she does is say mean things about other people. Or she may betray you after years of friendship.

Your first impression is often all you have in business and situations like speed dating. So, trust it. Your first impression is most likely correct, so act on it if you do not have time to get to know the person further.

Red Flags

Some major red flags automatically tell you that someone is toxic. When you observe these traits or habits in someone, you know that someone is not good to be around. Run away when you spot these red flags. Do not somehow rationalize or justify these traits, as they are serious signs of underlying emotional issues or sociopath.

Easy to Anger

A person who is easily ignited has anger problems. One day you will probably be the victim of his anger if you are not careful. Therefore, you should avoid people who are angered easily.

A history of violence is one sign that a person is easy to anger. Another sign is if he seems to demonstrate an angry posture. He will talk about fighting people or getting angry. He will immediately appear angry over the tiniest setbacks, such as his food being late at a restaurant.

Blaming Others

Right off the bat, you will notice if someone frequently blames others for what is wrong in his life. He will tell you all about how he is a victim. He will complain about how his ex-spouse cheated on him and brought about the divorce, he will blame getting fired recently on the fact that his former boss is just a huge jerk, and he will blame his recent car accident on the other stupid driver. Nothing will ever be his fault. He will claim that everyone else is responsible for his problems. And he will have plenty of problems to talk about. He will always be a victim.

Someone who plays the victim will probably one day accuse you of doing something wrong to him. He will never see how he is at fault. He will certainly never own up to his bad actions or offer you any kind of apology.

Constant Complaining

A very negative person will just ooze that negativity through his speech. He will constantly complain about everything. It will appear as if the world is against him and nothing in life is good or worth doing. Just being around this person too long will make you feel depressed.

Sadly, many people are like this. They only see the bad in life. You can assume that a person like this will only bring you down. You will never be able to lighten someone like this up because he chooses to stay depressed.

Gossiping and Two-Facing

Some gossip is just human nature. Once you know someone well, a little bit of gossip now and then is normal. It is not a warning sign.

But when you first meet someone, the first thing you hear should not be a bunch of gossip about other people. A person who sits there talking about everyone else has a gossiping problem. He is two-faced. Don't be fooled and think that you are the only one that he gossips to. Once you leave the room, he will start gossiping about you.

If someone gossips a lot, you want to watch what you say around him. You do not want to reveal too much, or it will become public information in two seconds. You also do not want to let his negativity sour you against other people. He will try to make you hate everyone else with the juicy, horrible details that he shares, but remember that gossip is rarely true. Even if it is, you do not have to be a part of this gossip's drama.

Women have the worst reputations as gossips. But men can be just as bad. Anyone who talks about other people a lot is a gossip. Be careful around such people.

Lacking Compassion

Have you ever met someone who laughs when other people fall? He seems to get some sick satisfaction from the suffering of others. Even if he doesn't snicker at other people, he never demonstrates any remorse or compassion. When he speaks about other people, he uses very callous and cold language. When you point out someone's bad luck, for instance, he will snort and say that it is the person's fault. This is the sign of a sociopath or psychopath. This person is very dangerous and certainly not the type of person that you want in your life.

The average person is capable of at least some compassion in conversation. He will feel bad when you mention that you are going through tough times or when someone falls. Someone who does not show any compassion and just ignores you or offers a callous remark when you say something that calls for compassion is not someone that you should associate with. If you associate with this person, never expect him to show you compassion when you need it.

Things to Read

What He is Driven By?

Various things drive people. They will usually show what drives them by talking about it. For example, someone might say that he wants to go out to pick up chicks. Sex drives him. Someone who frequently talks about money and making money is driven by financial security and wealth. Someone who talks about socializing a lot is an extrovert who is driven by having social interaction.

What drives a person can indicate what he wants from you. Read a person's language to gather clues about what he wants in life. His drive can indicate why he is seeking any relationship with you, either professionally or personally. It also indicates what is important to him. If your goals align with his, then a relationship is a great idea. Otherwise, you may want to steer clear of this person.

What Feeds His Ego

Watch a person's ego to find out what feeds it. A lot of people are fed by accomplishments, such as making money or finishing a tough marathon. Some people are fed by flattery and being the object of desire. Some people are fed by sex and interactions with the opposite sex. What feeds someone's ego is apparent by what he talks about the most and what makes him smile.

Also, watch his responses to life situations. If a member of the opposite sex flirts with someone and his or her ego blossoms, you can assume that they have low self-esteem and require lots of sexual attention to feel good. If he brags about his boat and other material possessions, you can tell that material success makes him feel complete.

If someone has a fragile ego fed by superficial things like material possessions and sexual attention, you can be sure that he has little confidence. The issues that come with insecurity are thus probably prevalent in this person. He will also do things to satisfy his ego and chase after things and make stupid decisions to keep his ego buoyed. Expect vices in someone like this.

But if someone's ego is fed by more solid things, such as his accomplishments or the love of his family, then he is probably a secure and reliable person with healthy confidence and wholesome interests. You can trust someone like this to be a more solid companion in business or your personal life.

What Stresses Him Out

Watch out for someone's stressors. Everyone has a source of stress. What a person complains about the most usually indicates what causes him the most emotional stress. If he complains about family, communication, commitment, and not always getting his way or not feeling loved, he may stress. If he complains about work, his work line and the tasks that he must do are probably not well-suited to his personality. If he seems to get quiet or upset in large crowds, you can assume that large crowds are not his forte.

Knowing what stresses someone out is very useful information. You can learn what to avoid doing around someone. You can become more sensitive to what someone does not like and situations that a person does not function well in. This is great information to know if you hire someone to work for you or begin dating someone.

What Pleases Him

People will go on and on about what makes them happy. You will most likely find out what makes someone happy relatively early in conversation. But you can also look for clues in what makes someone smile or what someone fixates on with dilated pupils.

This is also useful to know. You learn what you can do to please someone. This can make you a better lover, friend, or even employer and co-worker.

How Does He Behave Under Stress?

How someone handles stress says a lot about how he will treat you when things get hard. Life can throw a lot of challenges your way, so you usually want people around to handle stress well. If a stressful situation arises and someone falls apart or gets fiercely angry, just know that he is probably not a reliable friend during times of stress. He is also not a good prospect in a stressful line of business. On the other hand, if he can remain calm and collected under stress, he is someone that you can rely on in the future.

Chapter 2: Personality and Birth Order

An individual's birth order can also reveal a lot of his or her personality. This isn't just restricted to pop psychology talk or mindless party chatter but based on a psychological analysis of how the person relates to their family members and how they are treated within the family based on their position or birth order. A person's family dynamics play a considerable role in shaping their personality. The role they fulfilled as children or during their adolescent years influences their behavior as adults. Our status quo as children establishes the foundation for our actions as adults. Notice how several times children born in the same family or raised in the same environment have dramatically diverse personalities.

Of course, other factors can determine their personality type in combination with a person's birth order. These factors such as the family's overall socio-economic status, education, number of children in the family, parents' professional achievements and more also impact an individual's personality.

Alfred Adler first came up with the theory of studying an individual's personality through their birth rank. He used it as a method for reading the behavior, personality and actions of his clients. However, it was Frank Sulloway who elaborated on the theory in his publication Born to Rebel. Sulloway's book identified five primary traits like extraversion, agreeableness, neuroticism, consciousness and openness.

The psychologist said that an individual's birth order impacts their personality even more than their environment. This means that the chances of two first-borns having the same personality type are higher than two children belonging to one family.

Here are some ways to read a person through their birth order.

First-Borns

Firstborn children are known to be responsible and ambitious leaders, who pave the way for others. They are original, creative and independent thinking by nature. Since they get more undivided attention and time with their parents, they have a clear edge over their siblings. Again, they are more proactive and take the lead when it comes to caring for the siblings, which makes them more disciplined, inspiring, responsible and accountable as adults. They are protective towards those weaker than them, and often lead others.

If parents place many expectations on the first in a household, the person may grow up feeling inadequate. This may not just lead to low self-esteem but also a weak personality that is marked by a constant need for validation, acceptance and approval. The person may end up feeling that they can never be good enough for anything.

Firstborn individuals are more goal-oriented and ambitious. They give plenty of importance to accomplishments and success. They thrive in or perform well in positions of authority, responsibility and maintaining discipline. There is an inherent tendency to be a control freak, while also being autocratic, dictatorial and bossy.

Because come first in the sibling hierarchy, these people are physically stronger than other children in the household, which gives them a marked dominant personality. They may have a high sense of entitlement.

First-borns are often high on determination, rule enforcement and attention to details.

Middle-born

Since they are caught between two siblings, middle-born develop a more complicated personality. They are neither given the rights and responsibilities of the older sibling nor the youngest sibling's special privileges. This makes them look outside the home for friendships and connections.

Middle-born often have very big social circles and are known to be excellent diplomats and negotiators. They are social creatures who function with a profound sense of peace and fairness. Middle-born are fiercely loyal to their loved ones and seldom betray people's trust. Typical personality traits of middle born children are flexibility, generosity and adaptability. They are known for their diplomatic nature and can play peacemakers in any situation.

Middle born children are primarily understanding, co-operative and adjusting. They also turn out to be competitive adults. Middle-born have a close-knit social circle who award them the affection they haven't received within their family. Middle-born are late raisers and discover their calling after plenty of experimentation, contemplation and deliberation. They are at the center of authoritative careers that allow them to utilize their power-packed negotiation skills.

Middle-born are generally social and operate with a deep sense of justice and fairness. They are good at teamwork and relate well with people belonging to multiple personality types since they have learned to deal with older and younger siblings. Middle-born display a more approachable nature, and they know how to wriggle themselves out of confrontations and conflicts. They are known to be resourceful and quickly master multiple skills.

Last Born

By the time the youngest child of the family is born, parents are well-versed in their parenting skills and more economically settled. This makes them less paranoid and more secure. They aren't excessively monitored, which makes them more independent and gives them more freedom. Last born persons are excellent decision-makers and operate with a high sense of entitlement.

The last born is known to be charming and risk-taking. They are independent thinking, original and adventurous. There is a greater tendency to rewrite the rules rather than following set norms.

Parents are less careful when it comes to their last born because they've already experienced being a parent, which helps them give more leeway and flexibility to the youngest child. Also, there are higher chances of pampering and indulging the child owing to a better financial status. Since parents are more relaxed and lenient with last-born, they don't turn out to be conformists. They are used to plenty of attention, and they don't worship authority.

Rather than walking on set paths, they will create their path. Since they've learned to compete with their siblings for their parents' time and attention, they are good at handling competition and aren't easily bothered by feelings of envy and insecurity.

Since they are more creative and independent, they thrive in careers such as standup comedians, painters, dancers, and authors. Typical personality characteristics include empathy, obstinacy, extroversion, manipulativeness, penchant for drama and more. These are your salespeople since they are glib and can talk themselves of almost any situation.

Sole Child

The only child doesn't have to compete with anyone for their parents' time and attention, making them self-centered. There is a tendency to think that everything revolves around them. They tend to spend a lot of time alone, which turns them into more original, resourceful, inventive and creative people. Sole or only children find new and innovative ways to keep themselves busy. By nature, they are more confident, self-assured, meticulous, expressive and firm. They express their opinions more assertively and confidently.

Since they do not have to deal with sibling rivalry of any kind, they are always used to having things their way. They become edgy and unsettled when they have to compete with others or things don't go their way. Sole-born find it tough to share the limelight with others. They almost always want to be the center of attention since they've never had to compete for attention at home through their childhood and adolescent years. Only-born are constantly seeking attention, respect and attention. In the absence of siblings as role models, their only role models are elders of the house. Since grown-ups become their role models, they grow up to be perfectionists.

Multiple factors impact a person's behavioral characteristics and personality. To make a more accurate reading of an individual's personality through birth order, psychologists offer some effective tips. They recommend analyzing a person's siblings while reading their personality since no two children in the same household ever share the same role. If one assumes the role of a caretaker, the other will invariably be the care recipient.

Other factors that are considered while analyzing an individual's personality through birth order are genetics, gender, social status and other factors (apart from their birth order). Together, these factors will help you make more accurate readings about an individual's personality than simply relying on birth order.

Chapter 3:   Handwriting

Every person's handwriting is known to be as unique as their personality. You can make an in-depth analysis of everything from their behavior to personality to the thought process. Graphology is the science of studying an individual's personality through how they write. Handwriting goes beyond putting a few characters on paper. It is about glimpsing into an individual's mind to decipher what they are thinking and how they feel based on their handwriting.

Here are some little-known secrets about speed reading a person through their handwriting.

Reading Letters of the Alphabet

How a person writes his or her letters offers a lot of information about their personality, subconscious thoughts, and behavioral characteristics. There are several ways of writing a single letter and every person has their distinct way of constructing it.

For example, putting a dot on the lower case "I" indicates an independent-spirited personality, originality, and creative thinking. These folks are organized, meticulous, and focused on details. If an entire circle represents the dot, there are pretty good chances of being more childlike and thinking outside the box. How a person constructs their upper case "I" reveals a lot about how they perceive themselves. Does their "I" feature the same size as the other letters or is it bigger/smaller than other letters?

A person who constructs a large "I" is often selfish, self-centered, overconfident, and even slightly cocky. If the "I" is the size of other letters or even smaller than other letters, the person is more self-assured, positive, and happy by disposition.

Similarly, how people write their lower case "t" offers important clues into their personality. If the "t" is crossed with a long line, it can indicate determination, energy, passion, zest, and enthusiasm. On the other hand, a brief line across the "t" reveals a lack of empathy, low interest, and determination. The person doesn't have very strong views about anything and is generally apathetic. If a person crosses their "t" really high, they possess an increased sense of self-worth and generally have ambitious objectives.

Similarly, people who cross their "t" low may suffer from low self-esteem, low confidence, and ambition. A person who narrows the loop in lower case "e" is likelier to be uncertain, suspicious, and doubtful of people. There is an amount of skepticism involved that prevents them from being trustful of people. These people tend to have a guarded, stoic, withdrawn, and reticent personality. A wider loop demonstrates a more inclusive and accepting personality. They are open to different experiences, ideas, and perspectives.

Next, if individuals write their "o" to form a wide circle, they are most likely people who are very articulate, expressive, and won't hesitate to share secrets with everyone. Their life is like an open book. On the contrary, a closed "o" reveals that the person has a more private personality and is reticent by nature.

Cursive Writing

Cursive writing gives us clues about people that we may otherwise miss through regular writing. It may offer us a more comprehensive and in-depth analysis of an individual's personality.

16

How does a person construct their lower-case cursive "I?" If it has a narrow loop, the person is mostly feeling stressed, nervous, and anxiety. Again, a wider loop can signify that the individual doesn't believe in going by the rule book. There is a tendency to rewrite the rules. They are laidback, low on ambition, and easy-going.

Again, consider the way a person writes cursive "y" to gain more information about their personality. The length and breadth of the letter "y" can be extremely telling. A thinner and slimmer "y" can indicate a person who is more selective about their friend circle. On the other hand, a thicker "y" reveals a tendency to get along with different people. These are social beings who like surrounding themselves with plenty of friends.

A long "y" is an indication for travel, adventure, thrills, and adventures. On the other hand, a brief cursive "y" reflects a need to seek comfort in the familiar. They are most comfortable in their homes and other known territories. A more rounded "s" is a signal of wanting to keep their near and dear ones happy. They'll always want their loved ones to be positive and cheerful.

They will seldom get into confrontations and strive to maintain a more balanced personality. A more tapering "s" indicates a hard-working, curious, and hard-working personality. Ideas and concepts drive them. Notice how cursive "s" broadens at the lower tip. This can be a strong indication of the person being dissatisfied with their job, interpersonal relationships, and or life in general. They may not pursue their heart's true desires.

Letter Size

This is a primary observation that is used for analyzing a person through their handwriting. Big letters reveal that the person is outgoing, friendly, gregarious, and extrovert. They are more social by nature and operate with a mistaken sense of pride. There is a tendency to pretend to be something they aren't. On the contrary, tiny letters can indicate a timid, reticent, introvert, and shy personality. It can indicate deep concentration and diligence. Midsized letters mean that an individual is flexible, adjusting, adaptable, and self-assured.

Gaps Between Text

People who leave a little gap between letters and words demonstrate a fear of leading a solitary life. These people always like to be surrounded by other folks and often fail to respect other people's privacy and personal space. People who space out their words/letters are original thinkers and fiercely independent. For them, they place a high premium on freedom and independence. There is little tendency for being overwhelmed by other people's ideas, opinions, and values.

Letter Shapes

Look at the shape of an individual's letters while decoding their personality. If the writing is more rounded and looped, the person tends to be high on inventiveness and imagination! Pointed letters demonstrate that a person is more aggressive and intelligent. The person is analytical, rational, and a profound thinker. Similarly, if the letters of an alphabet are woven together, they are methodical, systematic, and orderly. They will rarely work or live in chaos.

Page Margin

If you thought it's only about writing, think again. Even the amount of space people leave near the edge of the margin determines their personality. Someone who leaves a big gap on the right side of the margin is nervous and apprehensive about the future. People who write all over the page are known to have a mind full of ideas, concepts, and thoughts. They are itching to do several things at once and are constantly buzzing with ideas.

Slant Writing

Some people show a marked tendency for writing with a clear right or left slant while other people write impeccably straight letters. When a person's letters slant towards the right, they may be friendly, easy-going, good-natured, and generally positive. These people are flexible, open to change, and always keen on building new social connections.

Similarly, people who write slanting letters that lean towards the left are mostly introverts who enjoy their time alone. They aren't very comfortable being in the spotlight and are happy to let others hog the limelight. Straight handwriting indicates rational, level-headed, and balanced thinking. The person is more even-tempered, grounded, and ambivalent.

There is a tiny pointer here to avoid reading people accurately. For left-handed people, the analysis is the opposite. When left-handed people have their letters slanting to the right, they are shy, introverted, and reserved. However, if their letters slant to the left, they may be outgoing, gregarious and social extroverts.

Writing Pressure

The intensity with which an individual write is also an indicator of their personality. If the handwriting is too intense and full of pressure (indentation), the individual may be fiery, aggressive, obstinate, and volatile. They aren't very open to other people's ideas, beliefs, and opinions. There is a tendency to be rigid about their views.

On the contrary, if a person writes with little pressure or intensity, they are likely to be empathetic, sensitive, and considerate towards other people's needs. These people tend to be kind, enthusiastic, passionate, lively, and intense.

Signature

A person's signature reveals plenty about an individual's personality. If it isn't comprehensible, it is a sign that they don't share too many details about themselves. They fiercely guard their private space and are reticent by nature. On the contrary, a more conspicuous and legible signature indicates a self-assured, flexible, transparent, assured, confident, and satisfying personality. They are generally content with what they've accomplished and display a more positive outlook on life.

Some people scribble their signature quickly, which can indicate them being impatient, restless, perpetually in a hurry, and desiring to do multiple things at one time. A carefully written and neatly-organized signature indicates the person being diligent, well-organized, and precision-oriented.

Signatures that finish in an upward stroke demonstrate a more confident, fun-loving, ambitious, and goal-oriented personality. These people thrive on challenges and aren't afraid of chasing these dreams. Similarly, signatures that finish with a downward stroke are an indication of a personality that is marked by low self-esteem, lack of self-confidence, low ambition, and a more inhibited personality. These folks are likelier to be bogged down by challenges and may not be too goal-oriented.

Stand Out Writing

If a particular piece of writing stands out from the other text, look at it carefully to understand its personality.

For example, if the text is generally written in a more spread out and huge writing, with only some parts of the text stuck together, the person may most likely to be an uncertain, dishonest, or mistrustful individual, who is trying to conceal some important information.

Concluding

Though studying an individual's handwriting can offer you accurate insights about his or her personality, it isn't completely fool-proof. Several other factors are to be taken into consideration to analyze a person accurately. It has its shortcomings and flaws. At times, people may write in a hurried manner, which can impact their writing.

Similarly, the way people construct their resume or application letter may dramatically vary from writing a to-do list or love letter.

If you want an accurate reading of someone's personality, consider different personality analysis methods like reading verbal and non-verbal communication techniques. Various techniques may offer you a highly in-depth, insightful, precise, and comprehensive understanding of a person's inherent personality.

Chapter 4: How to Avoid Mistakes

Mistakes. You think about them, talk about them, and lastly obsess

regards to them. These mistakes help a human being to grow but, side by side they are very much embarrassing, shameful, and put companies to a great loss.

Everyone has the same old habit which they want to change by doing some mistake or the other. It is a part of human psychology to repeat the same behavior again and again. Therefore, changing the old behavior can be difficult but not impossible. It can only be eradicated by proper planning and staying positive while doing any work.

In human life, mistakes are very common things by which he/she learns a lot.

Sometimes when we work too much, some careless and silly mistakes will happen, especially when doing your best. There is a number of examples of mistakes like sending an e-mail to the wrong person, overlooking a balance sheet, not ready for a presentation, and innumerable others.

Indeed, the person who is good at analyzing people easily judges whether they have done some mistake or not by non-verbal communication channels.

Here you will come to know "How to avoid mistakes at work"?

First of All, Acknowledge a Mistake

Until and unless you fully appreciate what exactly has happened, till then it is impossible to avoid it. Some of the individuals are very hard at failure but forgot to re-examine what is to be done to avoid the mistake next time. So, keep these things in mind before doing any work: -

Don't be overconfident while doing any work as it leads to missing any information and you will tend to make a mistake

There are many bad habits which can be the reason of mistake so avoid any bad habit

Doing mistake means you are trying your best but do overdo it

Concentrate on What You Are Doing

Just focus on your tasks and projects firsts. At the office, make work your priority and avoid any kind of activity while doing office work. On the other hand, don't be a multitasked as it kills the overall productivity.

Moreover, start the work from the smallest and easy task and then take up a tough one.

Furthermore, at the start of the day give importance to those tasks which are significant.

Don't Fear Mistakes

This is one of the essential points to keep away from doing mistakes. The reality is in the fear of making a mistake, you try to be perfect but forget that only you learn a lot by mistakes.

In a study, it is considered that the human brain before doing any work sends a warning signal to prevent us from repeating the same mistakes again and again.

However, making mistakes is a good thing which eventually allows analyzing themselves and others; but, up to some limit. So, do your work keeping past mistakes in mind.

Avoid Distraction

Don't get distracted while doing any of the office work as it is prone to mistakes. Distraction can take away your attention and make you jump between the task and the project. On the other hand, it also lowers down the overall productivity from your behalf.

Moreover, they create confusion and your attention will get split between two works. One essential step while doing office work is just put your phone aside as it is one of the most distracting things because of which end number of mistakes can happen.

Take the Breaks at the Appropriate Time

If you work continuously then, it will harm your brain and it will not function in the right way. According to Harvard Business Review, if the person does overwork then the aging process will move faster, resulting in memory and thinking skills.

So, to avoid this take some precautions like: -

Take some break while doing work and relax for some time

Talk to friends and relatives as it makes your brain relaxed and offer you a positive attitude of doing work

When you take a break in work, do something refreshing as it will activate your brain

Ask Doubts and Questions

The main reason for making a mistake is having doubts about the assigned work because of their ego or too afraid to ask. Most individuals think that what other people will think if they ask any doubt; but they forget that if they do some mistake what another person will say about you. Now you can well assume that which one is essential for you.

Therefore, try to ask whatever comes in your mind with regards to the work. This, in turn, will help learn more about the task and can be very useful in completing your work on time without any mistakes.

Try to Make a Checklist

Checklists will help you keep track of all the steps you will do while completing a task. By following this process, your work will be full-fledged without any errors because you have taken care of every step by rechecking them repeatedly.

This checklist is also crucial for those who are multitaskers and want to do multiple works simultaneously. For them, it is very essential. And one of the crucial things in multiple tasking is don't leave any work incomplete otherwise you will lose the grip on that work.

Do External Proofreading on Your Behalf

As an individual, if you have given your best in doing work then also cross-check the work again and again so that there are no chances of mistakes.

Try to analyze your work by taking the help of your manager, supervisor, or any experienced colleague.

Notwithstanding, getting a second eye on the work is a good method of improvising your work. And also, they make you understand overlooked errors which you are not able to understand.

Be Clear with Regards to Your Role in the Organization

Do you know- what is the role your company has given you?

It is essential to know this otherwise you will mess up all the things to complete every task.

On the other hand, surety of work offered to you makes you comfortable and will be mistake-free.

However, if you have any doubt about your duties and responsibilities then ask your boss to define it, and after that things will work much easier. In this case, there are no chances of errors.

Learn from Every Mistake Which You Will Do

In case any mistake is done by you, don't blame it on others rather take the responsibility of that mistake for what you have done.

As an employee of any organization, learn from every error done by you and from others. Always note all the mistakes done by you and by your colleagues and do the best effort not to repeat it. Moreover, when you show a positive attitude towards the mistakes, it will become a stepping stone to your success.

Indeed, this process makes you analyze yourself and others which are best for making strong relationships.

Always Find the Root of the Mistake

Every human being makes mistakes but once it is done, taking precautionary measures to not repeat is mandatory.

If you want that this mistake will not happen again, try to determine the root cause of the mistake.

After that think deeply about that issue and what are the steps you can take to prevent it further in the future. This will also help you to analyze your capability to get successful in life while observing others.

Try to Have a Healthy Conflict

A single human being does mistakes; but, in some cases, it might be due to conflicts between colleagues because of clashes in ego and opinions.

Make sure that you build a healthy relationship with each other so that every solution can be sought with colleagues' help. Make yourself friendly and make a good rapport within the organization.

We all are human and mistakes are our part of life. The person who learns from the mistakes and tries not to repeat it is the best human being. So, with your own mistakes, you can analyze other individuals also the way they react and act to the mistakes and judge their personality.

Chapter 5: How to Detect Trickery, Con, And Deceits?

Detecting trickery, con, and deceits is not an easy project because many police detectives usually apply some precarious strategies to analyze suspects' statements and reports. This strategy is called statement analysis, and it can help them to detect lies in the report. The detectives will examine the words and comments made by the suspects in writing independently while checking for any facts.

This process will help them discern the truths in the statement, and if there is any omitted information, such omission will be queried. Some intentional additions made to the report aimed to conceal the truth, but a careful investigation will reveal such lies and deal with it subsequently.

Detectives usually follow some processes while analyzing reports, especially if they are discerning a classic truthful statement based on the norms. They will be able to analyze these norms and even detect any deviation from the typical, resulting in fabricated statements. FBI detectives apply some steps in making a concrete analysis of every information supplied by suspects to detect deceits in disguise.

According to the FBI Law Enforcement Journal of 1996 entitled, "What Do Suspects Words Reveal?" Detectives endeavor to identify any aberration from the standard and even analyze what is distinctive of an ingenious report.

Let us analyze some concrete signs of deceit and falsehood that criminally-minded persons use to wiggle their way out of a case.

Making Uncertain Remarks and Expressions

A suspect will try to dodge the criminal intelligent officer's interrogations by making uncertain and vague statements. Such expressions are meaningless and full of ambiguities and doubts. However, when criminals make this type of reports, they tend to seek for ways to make additions or amendments later on.

Some of the expressions and words that could deceive an interviewer are supposed, almost, thought of, about, maybe, could have, guess, perhaps, approximately, and sort of.

Talking About Past Events with Present Tense

Liars and Cheats speak of past events using the present tense. This attitude connotes that such persons have taken time to practice and meditate on such incidences in their minds to use present 'action' tenses. The ultimate intention of using these types of tenses and statements is to deceive and con the listeners and judge alike in a court of law. An example of this type of statement could be seen in the following lines, "When I got to the office this morning, I met nobody at the reception room, but I find out that the window is open. As I approach director's office, I notice his door open, and his laptop is nowhere to be found".

The beginning of this statement contains correct tenses, but towards the end, the speaker intentionally diverted to wrong tenses to pull the wool over the detectives' eyes. However, their ability to identify this anomaly in the suspect's speech will help them know that his statement is flawed.

Responding to Questions with Their Questions

Responding to questions with questions is another smart way employed by tricksters to dodge giving investigators the right answers. They know that blatant lies could be detected after investigations; therefore, they try to camouflage the truth by masking it with carefully crafted questions. Some of these questions include "How can I take money out of my drawer and claim that it was stolen?" "Do I look like a thief?"

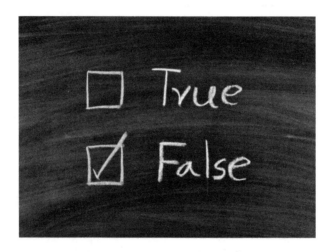

No Reference to Themselves in Their Statement

If you want to detect trickery, con, and deceits from a suspect's statements, you will notice that he will not be referring to himself in his speeches rather he will prefer to use neutral comments. For example, "The office was not locked" or "The money was taken away" However, the statement should have been, "I did not lock the office" or "I took the money away" if he wants to be truthful and refer to himself.

In the statements above, the suspect commented in the passive voice instead of in the active voice.

Convincing Interviewers with Oaths

The use of swear words, oaths, and pledges are the deceptive ways liars and fraudsters employ to manipulate or deceive investigators. They use these tactics to convince everybody that whatever they are saying is nothing but the truth. Some of the anomalous expressions that they use are "Let God be my witness," "I can swear," "on my honor," and "I cross my heart."

On the contrary, truthful persons don't have to use any cuss word to prove themselves, but they believe that their words' authenticity will prove their innocence.

The Average Number of Words per Sentence

The average number of words per sentence is determined by the total number of words in a report divided by the total number of sentences. This is also regarded as "mean length of utterance."

Most persons tend to use longer sentences to analyze issues in a statement. However, some sentences contain about fifteen to twenty words making them longer than a standard phrase.

A Truthful Sentence Should Contain the Narrative Balance

A truthful statement made by a suspect describing an event should have the 'narrative balance.' In a narrative statement, you should expect to see the prologue, main action, and epilogue. The 'prologue is the beginning part of the narrative describing how the event began or explaining the causes of the issue at hand while the 'main action' expresses the incident that occurred as it happened. Then, the epilogue is that part of the statement that expresses how the incident ended.

Experts have argued that the percentage indications of the whole narrative should be as follows: prologue should be up to thirty percent long, the main action should be forty percent long, while the epilogue should be thirty percent long. Moreover, they further argued that any part of the statement that does not meet up to the percentage mark is indented and should be further analyzed as important facts could have falsified the whole report.

Simple and Brief Statements Indicate Falsehood

One of the ways to detect a false report is by the brevity of the statement. In most cases, truthful occurrences are narrated in detail, but false reports are usually modeling with no analysis. It is also a known fact that accurate statements do not answer the question at hand but go into other aspects of the story's causes and effects to project nothing but the truth in the event.

However, liars and deceivers tend to evade the truth about the statement and tell just what they know can help them to escape judgment and penalty

Deception Entails Talking About Intended Actions

When suspects talk about proposed actions without saying that they did such things it becomes an allusion or merely a suggestion. For instance, a student answering a question concerning a missing book in the school library but does not want to state that he or she stole it, said, "I decided to go to the library and borrow some books whenever I had assignments to do. Yesterday, I got to the library, but the librarian was away, I tried to wait due to my project's urgency, but he was nowhere to be found. After checking the books in his absence, I left the library to complete my project.

Now, from the preceding, did the student meet the librarian? Did he wait for him to come back? Did he take any book from the library in the absence of the bookkeeper? The student narrated all these incidences without stating that he stole any book from the library. This is called 'allusion of actions' whereby the suspect talked about all he did without saying that he was culpable in the case.

Making Euphemistic or Vague Statements

Euphemistic remarks are made to present the suspect in a favorable and auspicious position in the case, to prevent hurting the personality of the person involved in the case. Examples of vague statements a subject can make to deceive the detectives are "the item was missing," rather than "the item was stolen," "I borrowed the book from the library," rather than "I took the book from the library,"

These are most ways an FBI agent or a detective can analyze statements made by a suspect to determine the veracity of such claims before conviction or acquittal.

Chapter 6:   What is Personality Development?

All individuals possess certain traits of personality that set us apart from the rest of the world. The mix of good and bad traits tells us how you respond to the situation. According to some studies, it is stated that these traits are genetic and remain fixed throughout life.

But according to some psychologists, they suggest that if you want, you can change these traits for the benefit of self or you can say for people.

So, personality is what makes a person unique and admirable. The personality of an individual consists of several components like temperament, environment, and character. With all these components' help, you can determine how that person will become or right now is.

Talking about temperament, it is a genetic determine factor that shows a person's approach towards the world and how they learn about the world. Indeed, there are no specifically meant genes for personality, but genes control the nervous system, which, as a result, has some effect on human behavior.

Another component called the environment is an adaptive pattern related to the surrounding of the person they live in. Some psychologists have researched that the first two components that are temperament and environment influence human personality the most.

Lastly, the third factor called character, which includes emotional, cognitive, and behavioral patterns, which are learned through experience, determines how a person can think, behave, and feel throughout his life.

Other than this, the character also depends on our moral values inherited in us through our ancestors.

Importance of Personality Development

To achieve success in both personal and professional life, a great overall personality is crucial in an individual's life. An attractive and renowned personality automatically influences every person. Whether it is a job, interview, while interacting with other human beings, and many more sectors, you must have certain traits and features that compel other human beings to say yes! What a great personality!

Nowadays, in every field, the personality of a person matters a lot. For instance- in the interview to impress the interviewer in business to influence the client and make them believe in you.

Therefore, the demand of personality has surged drastically over time. These days with the advent of personality, every school is careful about it, and they make their students a perfect example where they can excel in every field.

Some years ago, the overall concept of personality was very common, and no one approached it. Parents also rarely gave importance to it. It was just looking good while wearing good clothes, which is more emphasized in a work-related environment. Indeed, the interviewer just wanted good working skills of the person and not interpersonal skills.

But now the scenario has changed a lot in this age of competition and economic revolution. Let's put some light on the various points of personality which are considered very crucial in personality development: -

Personality Development Inculcates Numerous Good Qualities

Good qualities can be in any form like punctuality, flexibility, friendly nature, curiosity about things, patience, eagerness to help others, etc. However, if you have a good personality, you will never hesitate to share any kind of information with others, which benefits them.

According to the rules, you will follow everything like reaching on time at the office. All these personality traits not only benefit you but also to the organization directly or indirectly.

Gives Confidence

Great personality tends to boost your overall confidence. If you know that you are properly groomed and attired, it makes you more anxious towards interacting with people. Other than this- in any of the situations, if you know how to behave, what to say, and how to show yourself, your confidence is automatically on the peak.

Overall, a confident person is liked and praised by everyone both in personal and professional life.

Reduces Stress and Conflicts

A good personality with a smile on his face encourages human beings to tackle any hurdle of life. Trust me, flashing a smile on the face will melt half of the problems, evaporating stress, and conflicts.

Moreover, with a trillion million smiles on your face, there is no point in cribbing over minor issues and problems which come in the way of success.

Develops a Positive Attitude

A positive attitude is that aspect of life, which is a must to face any hard situation and one to one progress in life. An individual who thinks positively always looks on the brighter side of life and moves towards the developmental path. He/she rather than criticizing or cribbing the problem always tries to find the best possible solution with a positive attitude.

So always remember, if any problem occurs, then take a deep breath-in, stay cool, keeping in mind the positivity anyhow. This is because developing a positive attitude in hopeless situations is also part of personality development.

Improves Communication Skills

Nowadays, a lot of emphasis is given on communication skills as a part of personality development. A good communicator always lives an excellent personal and professional life. Indeed, after your outer personality, the first impression tends to fall on another person is what you say and how you say it.

Verbal communication of the person makes a high impact on another person. Individuals with good communication skills ought to master the art of expressing thoughts and feelings in the most desired way.

Helps You to Be Credible

It is a good saying that you cannot judge a book by its cover, which also applies to a person. Means people judge a person from their clothing and how it is worn. Therefore, dressing plays an essential role in the personality of an individual.

So, be careful while picking up clothes for yourself. It doesn't mean you will buy expensive clothes, but they should be perfect and suit your personality.

How to Develop a Personality

So, there are multiple characteristics on which an individual has to work while developing his personality. Here you will know some tips on developing personality: -

Be a Good Listener

If a person has good listening skills, they can make another person feel important in front of them, so be a good listener.

Take an interest in reading and expanding your horizons

The more you learn about various aspects, the more you become famous in your personal and professional life. So, read more and cultivate those interests in yourself, which make you stand in front of others with confidence.

On the other hand, when you meet people, you can share things with the individuals by making them flat.

Dress Up Well

While going to the office, party, or on any other occasion, wear a dress according to that which suits you. Good looks no doubt add to your personality, but what matters is how you dressed up for any occasion. Thus, dressing sense plays a very crucial role in personality development and building confidence.

Observe the Body Language

While interacting with people, try to use positive gestures, which make another person comfortable and relaxed. Some studies stated that 75% of the work is done by verbal communication in which another person judges a person's personality.

So, keep an eye on body language.

Remain Happy and Light-Hearted

Try to see the joy in the world and every work that you do. Spend precious and laughing with others so that you feel happy. Always appreciate people in one way or the other. So, smiling and laughing plays a significant role in making your personality awesome.

Stay Calm in Tensions

Some people have a good personality until and unless they come across some tense situations. Don't be that kind of person who becomes angry in tensed issues and shouts on everybody. Therefore, be relaxed and stay cool while finding out the best possible solution for a problem.

Develop Leadership Qualities

It is believed that good leaders have an excellent personality that can impress another person easily and effectively. However, leadership skills don't mean giving orders to subordinates. Rather, it means how well you can as a leader manage your subordinates to accomplish any task. Indeed, work hard to set an example for them who work with you so that if in the future they will get a chance to work with you, they will feel very excited.

Work On Your Inner Beauty

Most people only work on external appearance, but when you behave or speak outside, everything gets reflected. So, it is true that the outer look is essential, but inner beauty is also very crucial to be a full-proof personality.

Indeed, it takes only a few days to change your outer appearance, but, sometimes it takes years to change the inner world. So, work on that, and you can see the difference.

Learn From Your Mistakes

As a human, mistakes are part of life which makes an actual individual. If you are learning any new thing, you are bound to make mistakes. Always get ready to learn from your mistakes while saying or feeling sorry. Saying sorry will make a significant place to make a respectful corner among your friends or colleagues.

Indeed, if you have made a mistake, forgive yourself and move on.

Always Make Compliments to Others

If you see that someone is looking great or gorgeous, don't hesitate to say something positive. This will make your image or standard up.

Be Original

The next essential step in making your personality awesome shows what you are. It is a very eminent saying that original is worth than copied things. So, follow this and be how it is; rather, pretending what you are not.

Other than this, one should not copy someone's personality. But, you can adopt some habits of other individuals who are good and help you in developing your personality.

Meet New People with a Smile

Try to meet new people who will make you aware of a new environment and culture by which you, as an individual, can learn new things. Moreover, it also broadens your horizons.

Make Your Own Opinion

The opinion is something that cannot be changed or stolen from another person. For example, while sitting in a group when someone asks your opinion, give them your opinion, which is unique and is for everyone's betterment. This attitude will make you more interested and stimulating to be sociable.

Get Out Of Your Comfort Zone

Be ready, and always get prepared to challenge yourself to learn new skills. Like for most people- learning new things is quite challenging work. But with a positive attitude and confidence in yourself, you can tackle anything.

Don't Give Up At Any Point

Whenever you try to do anything and fail, give yourself a second chance to improve it. So, don't give up at any cost and try, try, try until you succeed.

Don't Make Yourself Aggressive

Well, in everyday situations, there are numerous assertive situations that make you angry. But, be careful because it is a big turn off to people, both in social and professional life.

If your nature is like pushy, then be honest to yourself and change it as soon as possible.

Don't Strive Hard For Perfection

Keep in mind that you don't have to attain perfection in any field because no one is perfect in this world. When a person is willing to show imperfection, then he/she is putting people at ease.

Evaluate Yourself

Evaluation is the best technique to change yourself towards positivity, so keep evaluating yourself regularly. In this case, take the feedback from your friends, colleagues, and other near and dear ones seriously, which will help you to improve gradually.

try our best to accumulate the most sought after and relevant techniques that are easy to understand and focus more on action than mere wordiness to be learned and implemented right away.

Chapter 7: How to Influence Anyone with Body Language

People are an open book. If you pay a keen attention to what they do and look at their facial expressions as they speak, you will likely get a better picture of their attitudes and personalities. It is important to analyze people as this gives you an upper hand in different situations. This will demonstrate the different reasons as to why you should analyze people.

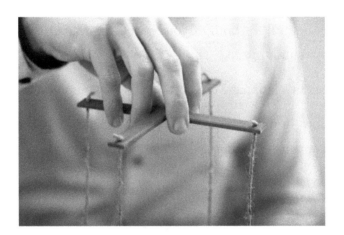

1.

Helps strike healthy friendship

A common misconception about the analysis of people is that it may lead to trust issues. That is entirely untrue. When you analyze people before becoming friends, you get to know them better and form healthy friendships. You know their likes and dislikes, and can even tell if they are genuine or not. With these facts, individuals who know how to analyze people will always get into helpful and healthy friendships and relationships. You do not want to get into relationships and friendships that will lead you to being taken advantage of. The only way to guarantee that is not just to take in the words said by the other person but also to tell whether the two agree.

45

2. Helps find a common ground

If you know how to analyze people, you can put that skill into arriving at a common ground. This is a skill that you will not just use with a few people. It can also be used while delivering vital speeches to various audiences. As you say something, you gauge what their reactions are through people analysis skill. When you realize that you have gone too far, you can backtrack slightly so that you all get to a common understanding. Getting to a common understanding means being at a position that is neutral for both of you, hence chances of getting into confrontations are minimized.

3. Helps speak in a language understandable to your audience

When you know how to analyze people, you can tell when they understand what you are saying and when they don't. You can easily see when whatever you have been saying hasn't been understood, even if the other person doesn't tell you that. For example, as a teacher, you could see from your student's faces that they are lost and require proper clarification. Similarly, as a parent, you may give your children instructions, but that doesn't mean they will understand whatever you said right away. Through the people analysis skills, you can gauge whether another person is understanding your communication style or whether you need to change your mode of message delivery.

4. Makes you dependable for advices

Your friends are bound to get into trouble from time and again with their boyfriends or girlfriends. Because you know how to analyze people, you can listen to their side of the story while analyzing them too and also get to interact with their partners before giving an advice. People tend to reveal more with their facial expressions. You can analyze these to get the hidden message behind their words. The advices you give are more likely to be genuine and helpful. They are based on facts rather than assumptions, hence helpful to the person asking for your advice. Even if your advice would not be followed to completion as you would have wanted, time will prove that you were right. That goes a long way in solidifying your position as a dependable person for advices.

5. You are always prepared

If you know how to analyze people, you will always be prepared for outcomes that would have otherwise been surprising. Whether you are getting ready for a meeting with the board of directors, or your juniors at work made a catastrophic mistake that they are trying to hide, you can analyze them and know it. We live in a world where however possess information has the upper hand. When you analyze members of your team, you can collect the information without them even knowing it. In case they were planning anything that isn't favorable to you, you can undo it before its occurrence. Let's say your boyfriend or girlfriend has been acting weirdly in recent days but they still tell you everything is fine. You could use your analysis skills to find out that they are actually cheating and even have plans to break up with you! They may think that their plans are well hidden but in real sense you already have the facts and just decided to play along. When they eventually decide to come out of the hiding and drop the bombshell, it won't be much of a bombshell.

6. It makes you more considerate

The fact that you analyze people gets you to understand why they may act in certain ways. You develop some sense of protection towards others, a protectionist behavior that the average person may not have. If you are the boss at your workplace or in any other organization and conflicts are brought to you, you will want to first analyze the conflicting persons before decide. The ability to listen to all the people will not be motivated by you having too much time but by the desire to analyze everything so that you do not make the wrong decision. During the analysis, important information is revealed to you like what would have made people to act in such and such a manner. Thus, as you start making the final decision, you will put all these facts into consideration. This is in contradiction to individuals who make decisions based on what they hear. The decisions of such individuals could even be biased and may end up punishing the wrong person. As a person with people analysis skills, punishment is not within your scope because you know sometimes people act not out of their will but out of a background force. This force is only revealed to you when you analyze them.

7. You get really smart

Not to brag but knowing how to analyze people makes you smart. From the many years of doing this, you wire your brains to think in a certain manner that other people's brains do not. The process has also led you to know the many different types of people on our planet and can form topics that anchor well with these. You form well formulated opinions on topics and can't wait to speak them out. You are the kind of a person who can deliver an electrifying speech on different occasions with various audiences. All you have to do is analyze the audience and choose the direction in which your topic should move.

Furthermore, the people analysis skills empower you to stimulate anyone's brain. Thinking, talking, discussing and conversing are your erogenous zones and anyone can tap into those in a stimulating way.

Having understood the other person, you know what you can say to get them stimulated and what to avoid as it could lag them behind.

Chapter 8: How to Use the Knowledge of Non-Verbal Language in Practice?

Pay attention to the gestures you use in everyday life - they are your main traitor; they give out your thoughts and feelings. Practically anyone will figure out your deception if you keep your hands at your mouth and hide your eyes. These bright lies are known even to a child. Therefore, be careful - do not do what can betray your deception. In order not to impersonate, you must very strictly monitor your hands, body, facial expressions. Follow the rule: no unnecessary movements. At first, it will be very difficult to do without hands, because we are so used to helping ourselves non-verbally in the process of speech, that it will be very difficult to get rid of this habit. But you have to force yourself; otherwise they will know your deception.

Unlearning to gesticulate and change facial expressions is difficult, but in reality, it will be even harder to learn to hide the involuntary reactions of your body. These include holding your breath, increasing heart rate, and trembling of the body. Some techniques allow you to hide these signs of deception.

You must train your body so that it does not betray your deception. Ask someone from relatives or friends to test you on a lie detector at home. Your partner should be at a very close distance from you and fix your pulse while holding your hand on your wrist. Let him control you in everything, watch your breath and changes of your facial expressions.

Then he asks you some questions. The first two or three questions should be the most elementary, for example, "What is your favorite dish?", "Skylark you or an owl?" that you will answer without difficulty. But the next question is provocative, for example: "Have you ever lied to your friends?" You can hardly answer this question without changing your face. The list of questions should be unknown to you; otherwise the experiment will lose its meaning. Continue the experiment until your interlocutor stops noticing changes in your condition. You can train long enough until you learn to control your body. You may not be able to fool a real lie detector, but you will hide your deception from a living person.

To repel an attack of a manipulator or an aggressive-minded person, you must first keep a distance, not let a dangerous person into your personal space. You will be able to maintain your independence and avoid its influence, if you leave in time or manage to keep it far from yourself. Suppose a person expects to greet you, when meeting you, and thus invade your space. You are sure that he has unkind intentions, for example, he decided to deceive or outwit you, and you should find any possible way to avoid of dodging hugs or kisses of foe to your intimate zone.

Do not allow a person, who has unkind intentions, to use nonverbal familiarities like tapping your shoulder or beating your cheek. Try to avoid such kind of contacts. You can take signs of attention from his side, but do it very carefully to avoid falling under his influence.

If you feel that a threat is emanating from a person, you should look away, look at another object. The fact is that prolonged eye contact with such a person is very dangerous; because an experienced manipulator can hypnotize you; convince you of something against your will. Therefore, try to look away; do not look intently at your interlocutor.

You can make a person understand that you do not intend to obey him; you do not want to engage in a long frank conversation with him. To do this, you can use closed gestures: cross your arms over your chest or put them in your pockets. You can make it clear to your interlocutor that you do not want with the desire to continue the conversation by constantly looking at your watch.

To impress, remember a few rules. The first rule is appearance: you must be careful, restrained in details, not too pedantic. If you doubt which style to give preference - then stop your choice on the classic version: it is always a winning option. Pay special attention to the accessories, they make your style unique; they talk about your personality.

You can rehearse your appearance in front of the mirror - practice your walk and salutation. Do you want to make an impression? There is nothing easier. Learn to walk properly. Previously, to make their gait and posture beautiful, the girls wore jugs of water on their heads. In our time, this tradition is outdated. But you can use a similar technique, not only for girls and women, but also for the stronger sex. Put a few books on your head and walk around so that these books do not fall. You should achieve the following effect: when you move quickly, no book will fall off your head. Gradually you can increase the load.

The gait of a woman is her personality. She can tell a lot about her owner. For example, the hips' active wagging indicates that the girl is too frivolous, trying to attract the attention of men. If a girl paces like a durable tin soldier, she is most likely unfriendly, unkind. The gait of a woman should be soft, smooth, with a "plastics of a panther before jumping." If your gait is not good enough, you should correct it.

There is a method of Marilyn Monroe, and from her walk, many men lost their heads. Remember that heels make a woman a woman. If you do not wear shoes with heels, then it's time to start. Legend has it that Marilyn Monroe had a heel on one of her shoes a little lower than the other, so she had to walk very slowly because of this inconvenience, she gently shook her hips.

A man should have a confident gait, with a wide step, but without waving his arms. It is advisable to stand firmly to give the impression of a self-confident person who knows his worth on whom to rely.

Greeting ritual is also very important when creating a first impression. When meeting you should follow the rules and norms of etiquette, for example, if you go to a business meeting, you should not hug your companion at the meeting or kiss on the cheek. For such cases, calm handshake is suitable. A handshake is a standard greeting ritual that can be used even by women in a business meeting. A handshake should not be too short, but it should not have a goal to seize the leadership position, for which some people deliberately hold their partner's hand for too long - this is considered a bad form.

A kiss on the cheek is a greeting that can be used when meeting two girlfriends or on a first date with a man. Make this kiss just a light touch. Some girls kiss the air not to spoil the makeup and do not stain your companion. But this is considered a sign of disrespect and a bad form. If you have bright red lipstick on your lips, you can warn about it or suggest a disposable tissue to wipe the print.

If you fulfill these conditions, consider that the victory is in your pocket. You will immediately be taken more seriously, and they will consider you a pleasant person in all respects.

Public Speaking Rules

For your speech, you choose a convenient place. Of course, if this is an organized event, then the organizers will do it for you. But if a crowd of people is an improvised rally or gathering, you should take care of where to get up. Find a place so that you can be seen from any position. You can climb a chair, or a table, or any elevation. You have to be head and shoulders above everyone for the public to feel that you have some advantage. You should be visible from all sides so that you can use the whole arsenal of non-verbal means of influence on the audience.

You must master the science to attract attention. How to do it? It is best to use non-verbal means. Your gestures should resemble the gestures of an actor on a large stage. For performances at public events usually use the following gestures.

You can spread your arms to open your arms. This gesture has a symbolic meaning: "I am your patron. If you have any problems, I will solve them. "To attract the attention of the audience, raise your hand and hold it until silence prevails. This gesture means: "Quiet! I will speak". This is a very bright, eloquent gesture that can be used not only at the beginning of a speech, but also in the middle, if, for example, you feel that attention is being dispelled.

Any gesture you use should be bright, big, and noticeable. Small gestures for performance in public will look like a curse, no one will see them. If you, for example, are going to use an enumerating gesture, then you should raise your hand to the level of your face, spread your fingers wide and bend them, making a big swing with your other hand.

Learn to use your voice properly. There is an opinion that for a large audience you should always speak loudly. You should not always resort to a loud voice — you will get tired quickly. Just speak clearly and pause so that your words are clear. In exceptional cases, you can whisper. The audience will think that you are communicating something important, uncovering a secret, and will listen to you.

To attract the group's attention, you must use special, chamber, gestures aimed at attracting the attention of a large audience. When talking to a small group, do not shout, do not swing your arms to gain confidence. We compared the behavior of a person, who performs in public, with the behavior of an actor: speaking in a group is akin to performing in a small stage, close to real life.

If you plan to say something important to the group members, you need to organize the group so that everyone can hear and see you.

If you are communicating with a large audience, of course, you will not be able to review all those gathered, but if you have a small group, you should take turns paying attention to each participant. Look at one member of the group, then at another, so that no one feels deprived of your attention. Visual contact will help you to feel each person, to notice the reaction to your words. If you look from one person to another, the whole group will be under your control. Also, each member of the group will feel that you are speaking specifically for him.

Chapter 9: Body Language and Persuasion

Persuasion is a technique that authors use to present their thoughts via logic and reason, to influence their readers. Persuasion may convince a particular action to be performed by readers or use an argument to convince the readers. It is an art of writing and speaking; writers earn their opinions plausible via logic to the audience, by demonstrating their credibility, and by invoking emotions.

Kinds of Persuasion

Persuasion has three Fundamental kinds:

1. Ethos

It's connected with integrity and morality. The viewer should know his comprehension of the subject and ascertain if or not a writer is not.

2. Logos

Logos includes logic writers utilize logic, reasoning, and rationality to convince viewers of the viewpoints.

3. Pathos

The method is pathos, which allure and communicates to the feelings of the crowd. That is contrary to logos since it poses arguments without using justification or logic. Many authors believe love, anxiety, empathy, and anger because variables that are powerful to affect the audiences' emotions.

Role of Persuasion

Persuasion is a literary technique. We do not discover it. Authors express opinions and their feelings by appealing to the viewers emotionally and logically. It is a method to acquire over the audience or readers. It provides them with an opportunity to research facts and helps pupils to unearth reasons. Students may comprehend the character of work while creating a comprehension of how their ideas and activities can alter and affect.

How to Persuade With Body Language

Your body language may help to get across your message, or it may send

the incorrect message. Understand what to do with your palms, your voice, and your own eyes to optimize persuasion and influence. I've covered to make messages that are strong in episodes the delivery is required by effective persuasion. Your body language can help you to get across your message, hinder even worse or even your sway, send the message. I will discuss how to convince and influence body language now.

Request in Individual

Do not send an email in case you've got an important request. It is far better to inquire. Your petition will be persuasive if it manufactured in person. Coincidentally, it is easier to say "no" into an email petition than somebody's face. Because you talk, but by seeing the body language of your conversation collaborate you'll be able to tailor your message. For instance, let us say when describing the advantage of your proposition, you see a slight "no more" nod. This is a hint your spouse and you may not agree, also you may utilize that information. Anyway, emotions and passion are infectious in individuals. Do not feel that? Has a laughing fit because somebody laughed? The purpose is that however many different points, smiley faces, or hearts you put in writing, they are no substitute for actual emotions experienced in person via facial expressions, voice, and expressions. Think about it's to listen versus studying it to the podcast. It is an entirely different experience. Persuading on the telephone presents challenges; you won't have the chance to see facial expressions or expressions of the individual on the line and you might not have their whole attention. So, if you are asking something of somebody, ask to fulfill in-person. Proceed to them. Invite them or to get java. Call a meeting if you are attempting to convince a group. When meeting in person isn't feasible, try out the next thing: video conferencing.

Assess Your Body Language

Remember that when you are meeting, the first thing that will be seen by dialogue partner is the position, and that is going to send an immediate message. Make certain that you comply with your grandmother's recommendation and stand up tall! It will make a difference. You have made the impression before you open your mouth. Eye contact is an important instrument in perception of trustworthiness. Use hand gestures to highlight and to encourage your messages and possess them. When you're certain, your audience is receptive, much more relaxed, and prepared to listen. Envision I'm standing tall in front of you, as it is logical, grinning using my arms to create gestures, and making eye contact with you. How would I perceive it by you if I stated the next? Imagine me saying the identical thing, but this time Arms folded, my mind down, poor eye contact, no expression in my head, and a voice that was none. What would your response be? What could you be thinking about me?

Be Consistent With Body Words and Language

The isue with this case is communicating that is inconsistent involving also my own words and my body language. The often-cited research on nonverbal and verbal communication of Albert Mehrabian shows the value of consistency in your speech. The listener must choose which to think if your body language and words conflict. Mehrabian's work indicates that if our messages battle, the listener almost always relies on to create their choice. If you are attempting to convince an audience of your body language, the company must support you. Shady gestures such as fidgeting, changing eyes, or smirking will excite suspicion. Open little gestures, arms, and facial expressions that reveal your audience will be engaged by emotion that is favorable and make you believable. Political debates are a fantastic spot between phrases and body language. You may observe a candidate grinning climbing gas rates or while talking unemployment. 1 candidate may say he respects another; however, the camera captures him scowling smirking, or rolling his eyes. With messages, we pay attention and quit listening to the words. That something as little as a smirk can cost the candidate votes and trust

See Yourself

A word of warning when we are anxious, we grin. If you describe a significant injustice or create a request for service or assistance, a grin

 will communicate the wrong message. Always ensure by assessing what your face looks like, the remainder of your body language and that your facial expressions communicate the emotions. Your body language is the most persuasive you're genuine. Body language is more difficult to control than simple words. Your body language will be persuasive if you're truly on your beliefs.

Chapter 10: Non-Verbal Signals of Aggression

The main gesture of aggression is a clenched hand. This gesture may have different degrees of aggression. If your interlocutor's hands are stretched out fully, while both are clenched into fists, then this is a sign of an increase in the negative in a person, he adjusts to fight. If the fists gradually rise, reaching the chest's level, then this is an alarming factor. The man accepted the fighting stance, prepared for the strike, and only seconds remained before the open manifestation of aggression. If your interlocutor begins to scratch his fists - he rubs his fingers with one

hand on the other hand, which is clenched into a fist, and has a negative attitude towards you.

If your interlocutor puts his hands on his shoulders - this is a sign of restrained aggression. This means that a person is ready to rush into battle, but is trying to restrain himself. If you do not intend to engage in a duel with him, then, having seen such a gesture, you must change the negotiating tactics: change the subject, change the tone.

A gesture characteristic of a person, who is aggressive towards you, is his hands behind his back with a wrist grip. This gesture is dangerous, since it is invisible to the interlocutor, if a person puts his hands behind his back, it seems that he is hiding something from you; perhaps this is a weapon for the upcoming fight. But even without a weapon, this gesture, in itself, is very dangerous and means that the person has unkind intentions.

To smooth the aggressive mood of your interlocutor, you can use the following non-verbal means. First, try to reduce the distance between you, use the tactile impact - touch the person. Remember, all your actions, movements must be extremely slow, so that your interlocutor does not take them for an offensive on your part. Remember also that if he is set up "unconditionally" aggressively, that is, he plans to fight in advance, regardless of your behavior, and then no means will help you. You should think about interrupting your conversation and going to a safe place, allowing him to throw out aggression on someone else.

A warrior's posture can indicate an aggressive attitude of a person: a person spreads his legs wide to feel confident that there is support under his feet. Its body is slightly tilted forward. As a rule, he tries to cover certain parts of his body in case you start attacking first. These areas are the most vulnerable places of a person. For men - this is the groin area, nose, and jaw. In women (although such a bright manifestation of aggression among women is not so popular, but still possible) is the chest area and face.

An aggressive gait is very bright - a person walks very widely, sometimes even jumps to get to his goal faster, while actively waving his arms, sometimes he can go running - this is a sign of a high degree of tension.

If you suspect your interlocutor in bad intentions, you should pay attention to his posture. If your suspicions are correct, then your interlocutor does not stand up straight, stretched to his full height. He sat up a little, pressed his head into the shoulders - he had grown into the ground, had become compact, now it is convenient for him to strike. If you are sitting, then your interlocutor can stretch the neck forward and shoulders back. Moreover, his head will be slightly tilted so that your forehead will be fixed in your direction, the hardest part of your head, ready to take your blow.

Aggression is a kind of protective reaction of the body. A person begins to show aggression as soon as he realizes that he is inferior to you in some things. It can be a result of anger, hatred, and envy. Perhaps your interlocutor is weaker than you in oratory, does not possess the talent of persuasion, and understands his intellectual inferiority; therefore, in the absence of other arguments, he desires to defeat you in an accessible way force.

The mimics of aggression is very active - these are eyebrows shifted to the bridge of the nose, swollen nostrils, staggering cheekbones, sometimes with creaking of teeth, very tightly compressed lips. These are mimic signs that your partner is very aggressive. Not always these mimic signals are reflected on the face all together, most often there are one or two signs. If you notice at least one of the above-cited signals on your interlocutor's face, be on your guard - he is not very happy about you.

Pay special attention to the look. In an aggressive person, the gaze eloquently tells that its owner is ready to tear to pieces his opponent. This is a very heavy, piercing gaze, so the predator looks at his prey in preparation for the attack.

If a person is aggressive, he usually raises the volume of the voice. And he does it unconsciously either to provoke you into actions beneficial to him, or to intimidate him. Perhaps your opponent does not have a competent verbal argument, so he tries to explain his point of view in other ways, that is, he does not resort to the power of the word, but the volume of his voice.

He is trying to "intelligibly", at a slow pace to explain his point of view. As a rule, he fails. He provokes you, tries to, as they say, "drive in": "Do I explain incomprehensibly?" All this is done to arouse fear in his interlocutor, to gain an advantage over the fight. He will try to provoke, putting into motion disparaging and caustic intonations, chuckles, grins.

For an aggressive-minded person is characterized by a decrease in voice tone, the use of lower tonalities, intonations, sometimes with hoarseness. Such voice changes are also intended to scare the interlocutor.

Sometimes the aggression does not have time to develop into a fight, and the person breaks into a scream. A person holding back aggression is in a state of intense tension. If you did not give him a reason for the use of force, this will not reduce his tension. And he still needs detente. Very often such a discharge occurs in the form of a cry. This is also a kind of non-verbal form of exit aggression. If he fells to a cry, then he is unlikely to use force against you. He just did not have the power to fight. In such a situation, you'd better wait until his anger subsides and he calms down.

You can try to relieve the stress of your interlocutor with non-verbal signals. Use the power of your voice to calm and defuse it. You must speak slowly, gently, as if to lull, put to sleep his vigilance. You can say anything, for example, to insist on your opinion, which put him off balance, but with all your non-verbal signals, he should read the following: "Do not be afraid of me. I am your friend. Take it easy. Do not worry. Better be friends with me - this is more profitable. " If you can correctly use your voice capabilities, then your aggressively-minded interlocutor will submit to you, moderate his ardor, and his aggression will go away or be turned to a different direction.

Chapter 11: Using Body Language to Negotiate

Whether it's a new car or a new job, knowing how to use your skills at reading body language to improve any negotiations you find yourself in can make a significant difference when it comes to the amount of money you either receive or pay in many diverse scenarios. Studies have shown that over 30 minutes, a pair of negotiators can trade over 700 different & distinct nonverbal cues. Here are some tips to guarantee that your body language will help things eventually work out in your favor.

Start poised for

success: When it comes to making the best first impression, studies show that those entering into a negotiation with multiple items in their own hands or on their person are statistically likely to begin the negotiation from a negative position. Ensuring you enter the room the negotiation takes place in as streamlined & ready for business as possible will make your overall odds of success much higher in the long run. It's important to take this momentum & keep it going by choosing a seat that indicates you hope this will be a collaborative process, not an adversarial one this means aiming for a chair that's at a 45-degree angle from that of the opposite party.

Take stock of the other party: Blinking, sweating, shaking, murmuring & erratic looks or gestures are all strong indicators that the other party isn't ready for the negotiation. While few negotiators are so obvious, it's important to take stock of the other party to see if you can quickly determine a baseline that you can use when moving forward. Be aware of negotiators who're too ill prepared, they may be putting on a show to lure you into a state of false security.

Keep eye contact as much as possible: During any negotiation, maintaining eye contact indicates trust, sincerity & openness both for you & the other party. What's more, failing to do so can make it difficult for you & the other party to build the sort of rapport that's more likely to lead to a mutually beneficial position. This doesn't mean you should hold the other party's eye contact indefinitely, only when you're speaking directly to them. Too much eye contact will instead make you seem overly aggressive & will make the other party less likely to give into your demands.

Lock down your facial expressions: Common emotions are tied to similar facial expressions the world over. This means that if you allow your face to give away your positon during the negotiation it'll be unlikely that you'll be able to prevent the other party from seeing your true intentions. Take the time to quickly practice how you hope the negotiation will go beforehand & consider what types of facial expressions would drive your specific points home. On the other hand, it's equally important to keep an eye on any expressions the other party might accidentally let slip, they could just give away key information that you otherwise might not be aware of.

Consider the personal space in the room: Studies suggest that the ideal amount of space between negotiating parties is roughly 4 feet. This essentially gives each party enough space to feel comfortable without providing either party an advantage that they can use over one another. Remember, if it's possible to gain any extra height compared to the other party it's in your best interest to take it. Likewise, if you're negotiating with a superior anything you can do to make the interaction less personal will ultimately work in your favor.

Act relaxed & confident: Even if, internally, you're extremely nervous about the way the negotiation is going either for you or against you, it's important to maintain an outward composure that's calm, collected & always in control. Ensure that your feet are firmly planted & that your arms & hands are loose & relaxed. Whatever you do, it's important not to twitch or fidget as doing either will betray your lack of confidence & cause the negotiation to turn back in the other party's favor. It's also important to avoid any outward nonverbal cues which signal discomfort in the other party. Depending on what it's in regards to, this can either be the sign that you just need to push your advantage or pull back to avoid losing the other party entirely.

Avoid smiling: In these situations, smiling is akin to giving in & saying that you're the weaker party in this exchange. Negotiating is serious business, show that you treat the current discussion as such & keep a calm face until the final details have been ironed out to your satisfaction.

Mitigating negative body language: If, despite your best efforts, the other party remains unwilling to accept your best nonverbal cues & continues to display negative body language, there're some things you can try to get them back to the comfort zone. One of the most effective strategies in this scenario is to hand the other party something relevant to the negotiation that they can hold & hopefully interact with. This will also get them in the mindset of changing their body language which will help to get their mind changing as well. Use this as a chance to take control of the negotiation & get the results you know you deserve.

Chapter 12:   Effects of Misreading People

The ability to read people and analyze them can help you become aware of your relationships and interactions. It becomes a useful tool that will help you build quality relationships. However, this is only a good thing if you get it right. Many times, people try to read others, and they fail. You get the wrong impression and make the wrong decision. Human nature is indeed complex. It takes a lot to analyze someone correctly. You must find the link between spoken words, facial expressions, body language, and so forth. Not everyone can get this combination right, at least not at the first attempt.

Misreading people is common, especially when you make assumptions or approach them with presumptions. You look at someone and form an opinion without giving them a fair chance to present their case. Body language is essential to communication, but it is also one of the easiest things to misread (Spaulding, 2016).

It is very confusing when you try to read someone but can only get mixed signals. Some people are so good at this. They throw you off their tracks. Others are just edgy, and in some cases, your inability to understand your inhibitions affects your ability to read people correctly.

Observers always look for consistency in behavioral clusters and clues regarding your behavior based on what they believe are normal or true for you or someone in your position. Perhaps you are used to seeing someone who is always happy, social, and outgoing, but one day, you meet them and notice something is off. They don't have their usual charm. The foremost thing that comes to your mind is that something is wrong. However, this might not be true. Perhaps they are just exhausted.

This is the problem with making assumptions of people. In most cases, you don't know half the things you think you know about someone, and if anything, most of the information you have on them is inaccurate or untrue.

The Problem of Assumptions

It is very quick to assume something about someone and misread them or analyze them wrongly. Assumptions form when your information is incomplete. With incomplete information, it is sensible to seek clarification from the subject. However, since you might be unwilling to do this, you draw your conclusions, filling in the blanks with distorted information that suits a certain persona you might have created.

 The information you use to complete the assessment is often your biased interpretation of what you feel, think, see, or have heard about someone. It might be from an earlier interaction with them or similar experiences you might have had with someone in the same situation.

With this information, you are ready to complete the puzzle. No one loves to be left hanging, so you complete the story and give it your perfect ending. The problem here is that the perfect ending is only credible to you and your mind because that is how you want it to be. It is not the reality. You make connections between the past and something that's happening in the present, yet these connections are unreal.

Assumptions are not the best way to read someone. Making assumptions over a rational concern can be disastrous. Imagine what happens if you make assumptions over emotional issues. Emotions and sensitivity go hand in hand. When you assume something about someone and the assumption triggers an emotional memory, the result will be disastrous, especially if it was painful.

Assumptions form because of your unwillingness to question or seek clarification when you should. They are dangerous for everyone involved, and this is why you should strive to analyze the situation better and get clarification to avoid misreading someone.

Laziness. Making assumptions is one of the laziest things you can do to read someone. You feel that asking for more information or waiting for the subject to deliver is too much work, so you choose the easiest way out.

You might get away with one or two assumptions. However, as you get used to it, you become careless in your assessments, and before you know it, you barely allow anyone to represent themselves fully. You jump to conclusions at your earliest convenience, and this becomes your plague.

Wrong Readings. You are making decisions based on the information you don't have evidence to support. This can only lead to more errors.

Responsibility. Another reason why you should stop making assumptions is that you stop taking responsibility for your actions. Each time you assume someone or a situation, you conveniently choose to hide your actions behind the most convenient explanation. This way, you don't have to own up to your mistakes. Instead, you can blame it on someone else for not going according to the script you assumed.

Holding on to the Past. Most assumptions are formed from things that happened in the past. Each time you have incomplete information, you take a trip down memory lane to fill the gaps. This is unhealthy behavior. Other than the fact that you end up with the wrong readings all the time, you also struggle to leave the past in the past. If you conclude from a painful event, you will struggle to heal. You must let the past go and move on.

Foster Negativity. It is quite unfortunate, but most assumptions we make about people are usually about negative sentiments. Since they hurt you in the past, you believe they will hurt you again. You cannot expect something positive from someone even if they try to change because you are holding on to a painful history.

The problem with this is that over time, the negativity grows beyond your mistrust and takes over your life. Your mind associates any actions from anyone else similar to what you experienced with negative sentiments. As a result, your view of the world is an unhealthy place where everyone is out to hurt you.

Create a Bad Habit. Assumptions are very easy. They are the easiest way out; they are comforting because they help you make a situation that didn't concern you, about you. You take center stage, and it feels good, especially in the short run. Instant gratification might work, but it never lasts. Since it is easier to feel good so fast, you get used to it, and assumptions become your go-to move whenever you cannot explain something about someone. This is how you end up creating a bad habit that ruins your friendships and relationships.

Empower Your Pain. The fact that you keep referring to painful moments when making assumptions only empowers the pain and makes it a part of you. You deny yourself the opportunity to heal and move on to greater and better things in life.

How do you overcome assumptions? To read someone correctly, you must understand them. Do not be afraid to ask questions. It is better to ask and be correct than ignore and be wrong about everything. Besides, when you assume something about someone, you do something with that information, and they realize what you think of them. Perhaps they held you in high regard, but your action challenges that perception. They see a different version of you that they might not like.

Asking for the truth is not easy. It can be painful at times, but it is better than not knowing at all. Your conversations with people are better and more productive because you allow them to express themselves. Everything is not about you anymore, but everyone else gets their moment.

Conclusion

It is not realistic to expect that most of us will develop the kind of extra-sensory perception that will make us mind readers. However, all people can learn to identify the non-verbal clues that others demonstrate every day.

Most of the time, we do not stop thinking about our body's language, what we transmit in non-verbal communication. It is even more important than the words we use, gestures, posture and facial expression reveal more than we can suppose or intend to demonstrate. To have control of these movements is to be able to pass the message of the emotions and thoughts in a balanced way, reinforcing the words with the gestures. Research indicates that only 7% of our communication is word-based. The body language is responsible for another 55% and the tone of voice for 38%.

A negative body language can convey weakness, insecurity. And we do not want our interlocutor to have that impression. Having the knowledge and mastery of our body makes a lot of difference in personal and professional relationships from the moment we recognize their power. A correct and upright posture requires training and corrections until you reach perfection. Sitting in the right way according to the environment, without overexposing yourself, demonstrates education. Standing without arms crossed or hands in pockets conveys confidence and security. Walking elegantly, even with very high heels, without much movement in the hips and without looking at the ground, projects positivity. The body should always be moved smoothly without sudden changes or drama.

Accelerated or aggressive rhythm generates a sense of stress and a lack of confidence. Carrying your hand over your mouth while talking or looking away from the caller gives the impression of lying. The look, then, is extremely revealing. No matter how hard we try to hide our emotions, it shows the truth of our feelings. How many times do we say one thing believing another? Those who pay attention to their eyes will realize how much truthfulness there is in words. An unfocused look can be confusing as if you are looking for a mental image for support. The famous twist of eyes denotes irritation and contempt. To contact the forehead means tension, doubt, or nervousness, a very negative point. Crossing one's arms away from the others represents the imposition of a physical barrier, that is, no opening as to what is being said. On the plus side, a firm handshake demonstrates confidence. Speaking calmly, articulating the words well, and maintaining tranquility, conveys credibility. Who believes in someone who does not express himself correctly, speaks in a fiddly way, without coherence of thoughts?

Knowledge and mastery of body language techniques add value to our relationships in any environment. Analyzing and learning how to deal with our gestural is a differential in social relations, there is no denying.

Reading people is a critical skill for anybody to have. This is because it will allow you to understand the complete message somebody is passing across when you are conversing with said person. This will put you ahead in your dealings with people and help establish you as a force to reckon with. Humans, for a fact, say more nonverbally than they do verbally. If you are to grasp what someone is communicating honestly, you should be able to read and understand their nonverbal communication.

Listening to nonverbal communication is an art that requires training to develop. This particular means of communication, as you now know, says, and hints at much more than you are liable to hear and get from having an oral or written conversation with somebody. For instance, body movement can be used to communicate a message in four different ways.

Being adept at the art of nonverbal communication requires that you master some five principles. These principles will allow you to identify nonverbal cues, but it will also help interpret them correctly. Without mastery of these principles, you will be prone to make mistakes where reading people are concerned.

Being a master nonverbal communicator also requires that you continuously work on yourself. For instance, emotional awareness, attentiveness, and constant practice, among others, are areas that you need to work on and strengthen if you are to become adept at reading what people are saying nonverbally.

Nonverbal communication has a host of benefits some of which are;

•to complement what is being communicated verbally,

•to deceive others into thinking something other than what you feel,

•to regulate what you are communicating verbally,

•to express your feelings and emotions on a particular subject and a specific person, and so on.

Another important thing you need to do when developing your nonverbal communication skills understands personality types. This will enable you to identify the motives behind people's actions, which will allow you to know what they are saying.

While being good at reading people is a great skill set, combining this with charisma is even better. This will enable you to resonate with people, empathize, and build great rapport with them. All of these are essential, especially if you are passionate about helping people become the best versions of themselves.

Speed reading people is especially important if you are a leader, a politician, or somebody who has a job that involves dealing with people. As such, you must learn and develop the skills necessary to become a good reader of people and nonverbal communication. This will put you in an excellent position to handle people and negotiate with them.

Body language can fill you in on the hidden bits of information that people don't want you to know about. It can let you know if a person is interested in what you have to say or if you are simply wasting your breath. You may discover a person that you thought didn't like you, actually does. You never know what you will learn through body language, and that's what makes it such a powerful tool. Use the ability to read people wisely, though. Some people are simply fidgety, so you can't assume that everybody who picks their nails is lying. Look at the big picture as well and make sure you know the person before you jumped to any conclusions based solely on their body language.

Lightning Source UK Ltd.
Milton Keynes UK
UKHW051946090522
402742UK00008B/199

9 781914 215704